OLD FARTS ARE FOREVER

by the *New Yorker's* Lee Lorenz

**Andrews McMeel
Publishing, LLC**

Kansas City • Sydney • London

09 10 11 12 13 RR2 10 9 8 7 6 5 4 3 2 1

ISBN-13: 978-0-7407-8502-3
ISBN-10: 0-7407-8502-8

Library of Congress Control Number: 2009926283

www.andrewsmcmeel.com

Some of the cartoons included in this book originally appeared in *The New Yorker* magazine/courtesy of www.cartoonbank.com.

Introduction

Just as people begin to look like their dogs, cartoonists begin to look like their people. This notion hit me one day when I looked in the mirror and discovered that, after so many years of drawing old farts, I had become one.

Over the years, I've chronicled us old farts from the boardroom to the bedroom, and from snowy Central Park to balmy Boca Raton. And despite my best efforts, we remain to the general public America's largest but least appreciated minority.

This collection may not change that, but at the least it's an occasion for us to celebrate ourselves.

All together now: "Old farts are forever!"

"Frankly, I'm sick of playing Tinker Bell to your Peter Pan."

"*You forgot someone's B-I-R-T-H-D-A-Y!*"

"When I said you should be easier on yourself,
I didn't mean you should let yourself off scot-free."

"Well, now that the kids are all grown, why don't we change our names, burn off our fingerprints, and start that life of crime we've always talked about."

"And then one day I suggested he go with the flow, and he went."

"The New Year is approaching, Miriam—traditionally a time of new beginnings. I suggest we use the occasion to dedicate ourselves to restoring that atmosphere of trust and mutual respect which characterized the early years of our marriage, and in that spirit we continue to work together toward what I sincerely hope will be an amicable divorce."

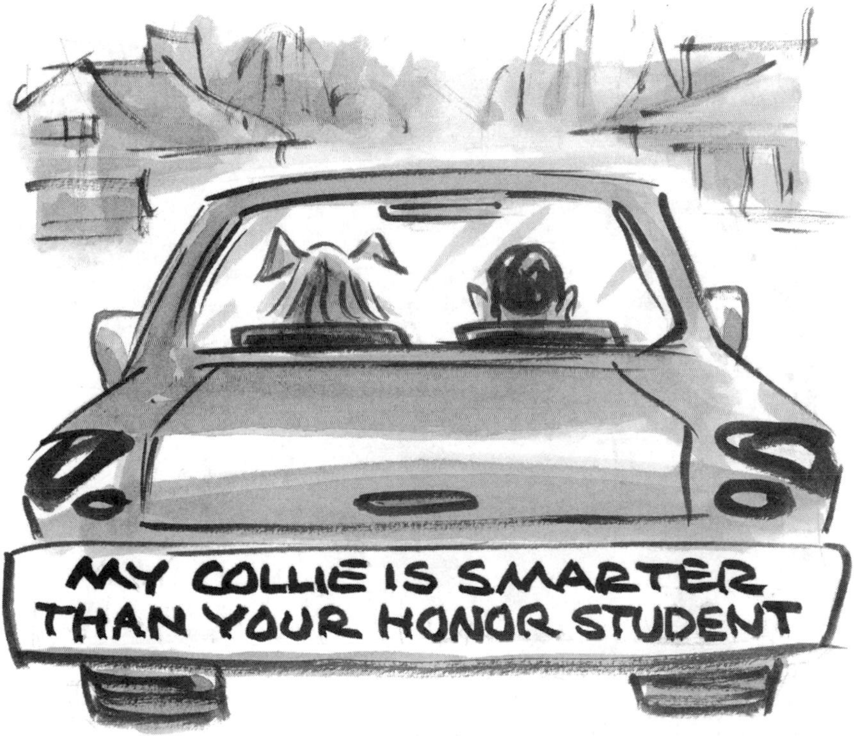
MY COLLIE IS SMARTER
THAN YOUR HONOR STUDENT

"My, my, Mr. Kessler. That certainly is
a nasty side effect you've got there."

"Lawrence has gone to a better place—South Miami Beach."

"I think you'll be pleasantly surprised by
how far your dollars go on Alpha Centura."

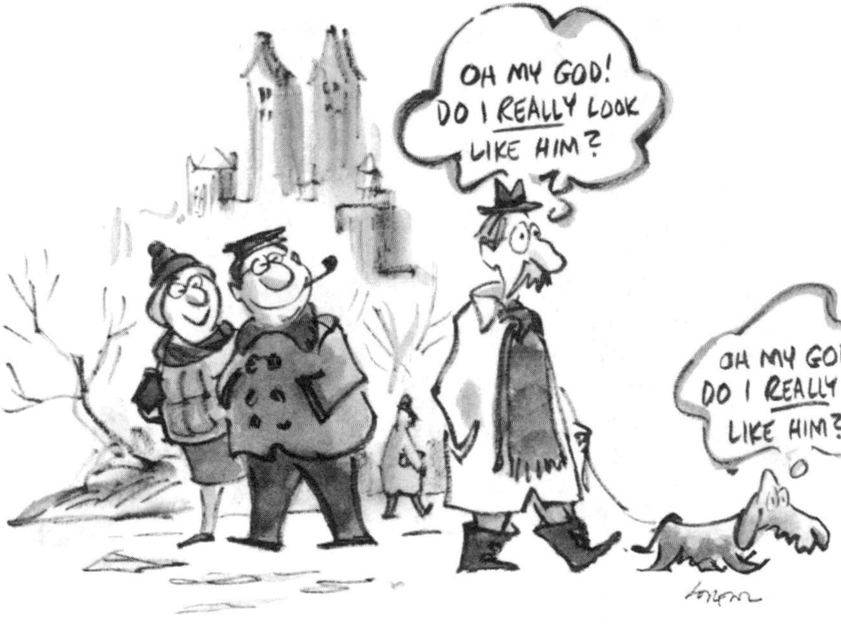
OH MY GOD!
DO I REALLY LOOK
LIKE HIM?
OH MY GOD!
DO I REALLY LOOK
LIKE HIM?

"*People don't notice you, Howard—why don't you grow a beard?*"

"Will you please stop saying we're the oldest people in line?
We're always the oldest people in line."

17

"That's Pemberton. He's part of the mess we
inherited from the previous administration."

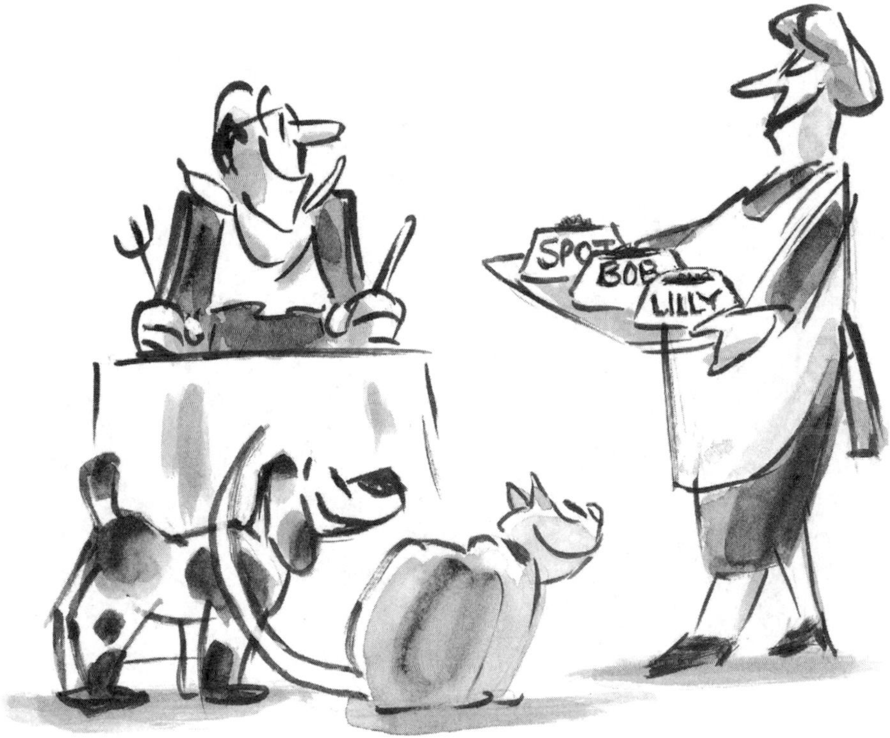
SPOT
BOB
LILLY

"*Between us, Flaster, there are two things
I never did understand—arbitrage and dames.*"

"Hold it! I thought ninety was the new middle age."

"Hey—who wants a six-pack when you can have a keg?"

"Gentlemen, it's a fake!"

*"The economy seems back on track,
but I'm not sure about Collingwood."*

25

*"Your mail, sir. I have taken the liberty of putting all the
envelopes that suggest you may already have won on top."*

"Really, dear—I just said that to see if you were listening to me."

"Haywood demands instant access to his cash."

"How come you never say 'Good night, sweet prince' anymore?"

"Of course, with my genes I'll probably live forever."

"Call in the family, Nurse McIntyre.
I think he's about to process his last words."

*"Now, if this *was* on reality TV I'd watch it."*

"Howard, I'm seeing someone else."

"Kids today don't care about anything except money—thank God."

"Honey, I'm home!"

*"And then one day he heard the president
urging Americans to 'go for it,' and apparently he did."*

THE FORKLIFT SCOOTER

"On the other hand, they take Medicare."

"It's certainly refreshing to meet someone
sixty years old who looks sixty years old."

"*Of course I still love you—it's called the Stockholm syndrome.*"

"I'm sorry, Mr. Brodner, but I'm afraid there's no way
we can legally change you from a Libra to a Sagittarius."

21ˢᵗ CENTURY PREVIEWS

HISTORY IS MADE AS THE MEDIA COMPLETELY
IGNORE THE **75**ᵗʰ ANNUAL WOODSTOCK REUNION

"He's no longer voice-activated."

"Just when did we become a same-sex couple?"

"And may we continue to be worthy of consuming
a disproportionate share of this planet's resources."

"I'm sorry, Son, but your mother and
I are moving back in with my parents."

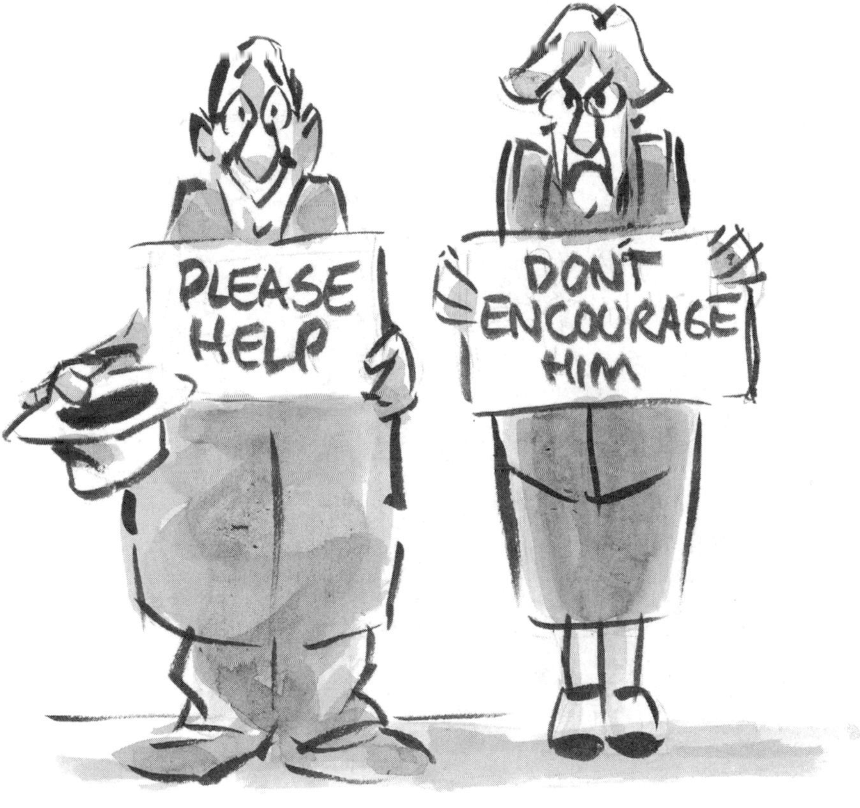
PLEASE HELP
DONT ENCOURAGE HIM

"Yeah, he's cute, but I'm too old for a fixer-upper."

"Tomorrow morning the Hang Seng index in Hong Kong will open lower."

"Why don't you do us both a favor and
stop saying how old you are in dog years?"

"*Very nice, but I understood there were to be bizarre sexual experiments.*"

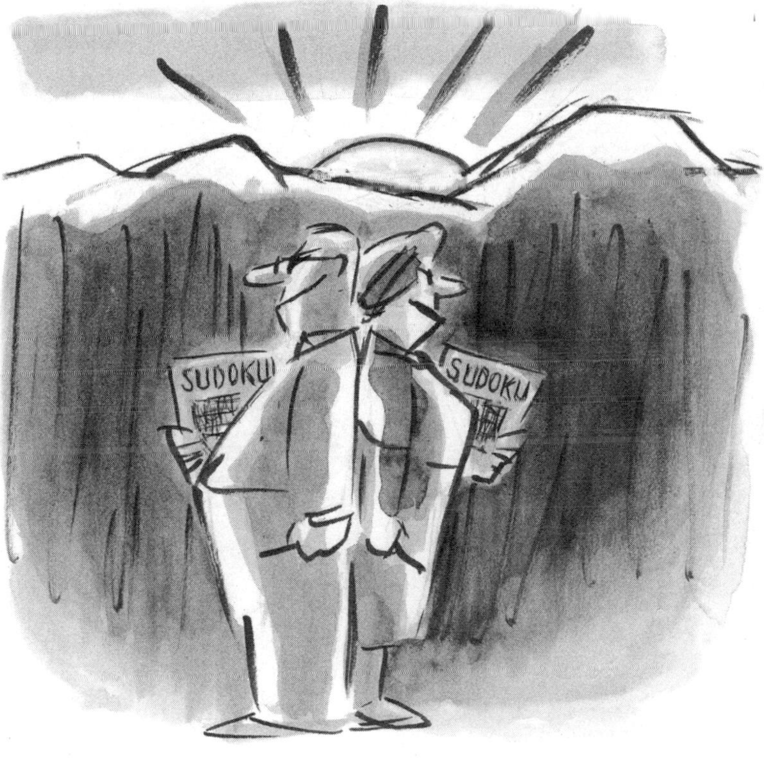
SUDOKU
SUDOKU

*"Why don't we make it simple this year,
and just give everyone the finger?"*

"I'm hanging in there, but I think Edgar is down to his last marble."

"Can't you give him one of those
personalities in a bottle I keep reading about?"

"It's the closure fairy."

"*If you're finished with the greed section,*
I'll swap you for the fear section."

"And if you prick me, do I not bleed?"

"Anything from the organ cart today, Mr. Harrelson?"

"Don't you remember, darling? It's part of your living will."

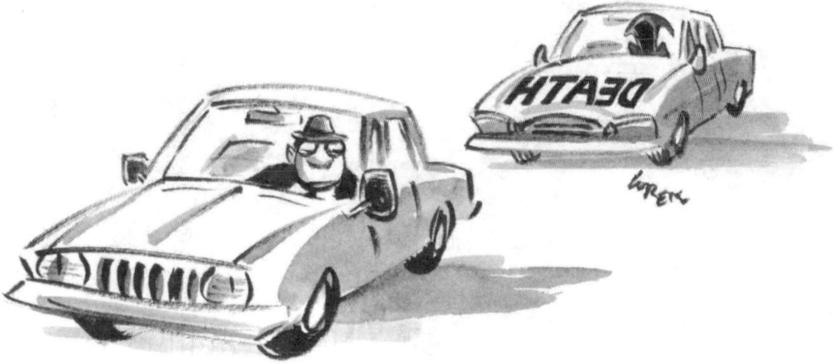
DEATH

"Gee whiz, Mr. Collins—two hundred and six isn't old!"

"Well, it looks like all those things,
thank God, you'd never live to see, you will."

"Is everything boring enough for you, sir?"

"Here's a new study suggesting we're better off dead than alive."

"If it's all the same to you, I'll let history be my judge."

"Wunderkinden come and go, but old farts are forever."

"*Is this the year, pumpkin? Good-bye, love boat, hello Elderhostel?*"

"And thanks for not sucking all the air out of the room tonight."

"Really? I never heard of a Cheshire dog."

"If you can hang on 'til ten,
there's something called 'Pimp My Scooter.'"

"Oh, Roger! You do have feelings after all."

"I'm not ordering any lunch, Caswell—I'm going to eat yours."

"For Pete's sake, Lucille, lighten up—it's only a sleepover."

"*They're an exciting new blend of Dacron, cotton, and Viagra.*"

"I said, 'I'm ready to make a commitment.'"

"*Aboveground burial was his last request.*"

"Take a load off, Leonard—we're watching
Generations X and Y duke it out."

"Forgive the mess. Warren just put everything into cash."

"No offense, darling—I just meant if
you wanted a face-lift I have no objections."

"If that's my wife, I'm still out crying in the wilderness."

"One day I just reached deep
down inside myself and there he was."

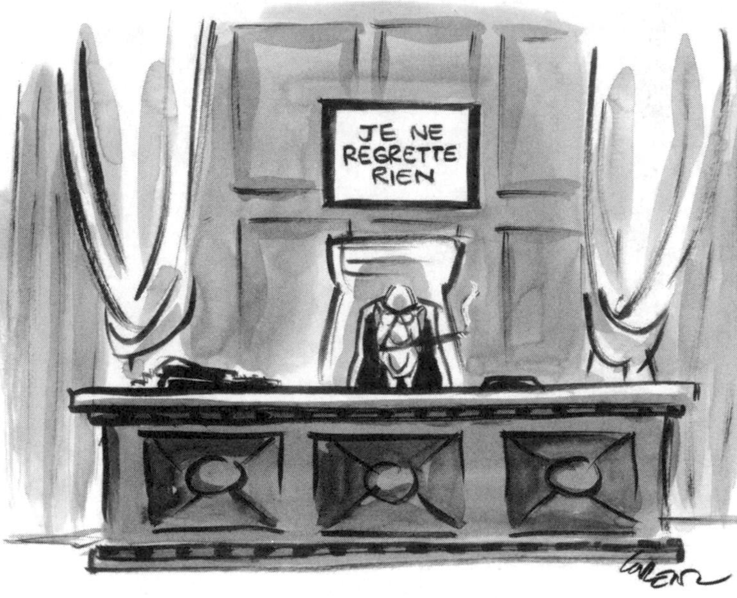
JE NE
REGRETTE
RIEN

"So what's the story, morning glory—boxers or briefs?"

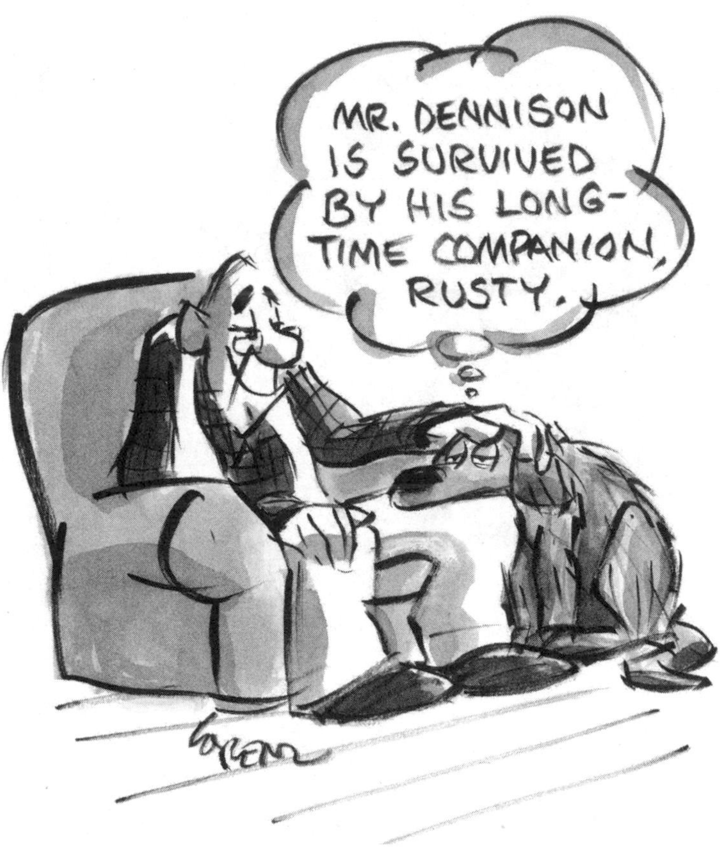
MR. DENNISON IS SURVIVED BY HIS LONG-TIME COMPANION, RUSTY.

"In Japan, Kyle would be a living national treasure."

"Leonard has always been, and will always be, a love sponge."

"Point well taken—but I just came here to get drunk."

"Archibald Monroe—I'll be heading Mr. Billings' transition team."

"*And to my heirs and assigns, I leave the war on terror, the continuing struggle for economic and social justice, and my share of the national debt.*"

"Seriously, Howard—wouldn't you be happier living with your own kind?"

"Really, Karen! He's old enough to be your husband."

"Call the family, nurse—he's about
to dictate his last letter to the Times."

"Well, what have we here? 'To Grandpa from Grandpa.'"

"If I'm not back in seven years, get a divorce."

"I, *too*, longed to find a cause greater
than myself—fortunately, I never did."

"That's my grandpa—Captain Underpants."

"*Well, we've licked taxes—that just leaves death.*"

"*Good old Henderson. Ninety-three and no one has yet abrogated his right to bear arms.*"

"That's the best you can do—'Time to call the gutter man'?"

"*I warned you it was lighthearted holiday fare!*"

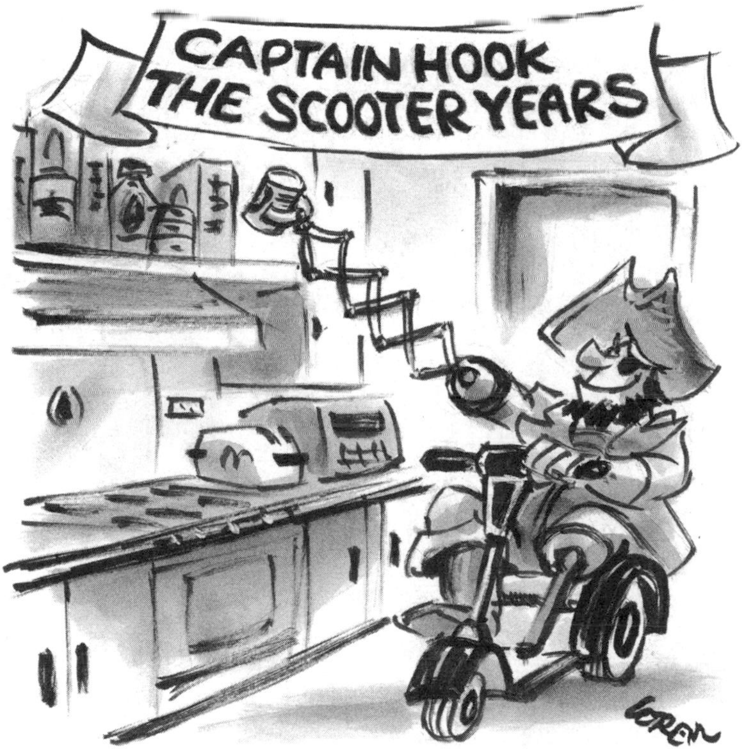
CAPTAIN HOOK
THE SCOOTER YEARS

"Sorry about this, but I just reached the hole in the donut."

*"You're not in material breach,
but you're not in full compliance, either."*

"I'm cutting him back to fifty milligrams a day."

"Granted, we're living longer—
on the other hand, we're out of it sooner."

"You're right—I'm not listening to you.
I'm reading the crawl on the bottom of your screen."

"Heroic measures and plenty of them!"

"There's a revolver under this coat, young man, aimed straight
at your laptop. One more phone call and I pull the trigger."

"It cost a bundle, but I can't tell
you how much better I feel about myself."

"So, what are you two up to these days?"

"I wish you could have known
Charles before his identity was stolen."

"Can he call you back? He's working on his list of
all the questions Larry King should have asked."

"In my ad, I lied about my age."

"Lately he's not the man I married."

"What is it, Ira, that draws man inexorably back to the sea?"

"In dog years you're an old fart."

"Howard lives his life, and I live mine."

*"Remember when the old guys were on
top and the young guys were on the bottom?"*

"Okay, I forgot our anniversary—so shoot me."

"Look after Foster, will you, Kendall? He's the new kid on the block."

"Thirty percent off on prescription drugs—that's it?"

"You've been eating again."

"Anytime you get tired of flagellating yourself,
I'd be happy to take over."